A Savior Is Born

Three beautiful adaptations of artwork by Frances Hook

Jean D. Crowther
Designer

Frances Hook
Artist

Contents

Instructions

Basic Cross-Stitch—Always be sure that your stitches cross in the same direction for a uniform appearance. If the bottom diagonal slants from the lower left hole to the upper right, all bottom diagonals in the piece should be worked in that same direction. (See Figure 1.) Use a hoop to keep the stitches uniform in tension.

Half Stitch—In some areas, the graph will show the symbol in only one corner of the square. To create this half stitch, work from the corner hole into the center of the square, placing the needle between the threads. Complete the stitch with a full diagonal in the color being used or complete it as part of the backstitch outline as indicated. (See Figure 2.)

Backstitch Outline—This stitch provides linear detail or emphasizes the design. Using one strand of floss, bring the needle up in the first hole indicated by the pattern. Place the needle down in the hole behind the initial stitch. Continue working one stitch length back on top of the fabric and two stitches forward beneath the fabric to form a solid line. (See Figure 3.) Backstitching is generally done last, after all other stitching is completed.

"Over-Two" and "Over-Three" Backstitch—To create a gentler line for the flesh outlines, two stitches have been created. These stitches will generally be used for the outside edge of the flesh profile. The terms "over-two" and "over-three" refer to the distance a single backstitch will travel over squares vertically or horizontally. (See Figure 4.)

When working the flesh colors, the area between the last complete stitched square and the line which will later be backstitched will need to be filled in with flesh-colored floss as designated. True half-stitches would be the wrong angle needed to cover these areas. Therefore, it is necessary to make short-angled stitches to fill in the area to be covered.

To fill in the area of an "over-two" stitch, begin at the corner hole of the narrowest part of the area and make a very shallow-angled half-stitch. The wider part of the area will need a steeper-angled half-stitch (perhaps with even the half-stitch crossed to completely fill in the area). (See Figure 5.) Leave the remaining stitches uncrossed.

The "over-three" backstitch area will be filled in the same manner. (See Figure 6.)

The backstitch color will later serve as the crossing stitch for the "over-two" and "over-three" areas. (See Figure 7.)

In some charts the flesh color of the child will meet another color in an "over-two" or "over-three" backstitch area. It will be necessary to fill in the flesh area part of each square with small half-stitches angled to fill in the designated area. Complete the remainder of that same square with small half-stitches of the other color. The backstitch should be worked with the flesh outline as marked. (See Figure 8.)

Feature Backstitch Outline—To soften the detail lines which outline the faces and hands, some liberty has been taken with the backstitching. Complete the cross-stitches of the design. Then using one strand of floss, backstitch on top of the flesh tones as indicated by the pattern. This pattern is drawn out to the side of the graph for clarity. The outline pattern will be on either the same vertical or horizontal line of the graph as the features it will emphasize.

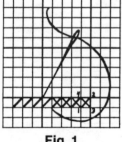

Fig. 1
Basic Cross-Stitch

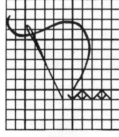

Fig. 2
Half Stitch

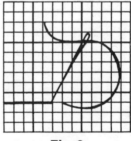

Fig. 3
Backstitch Outline

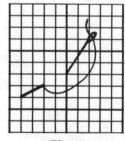

Fig. 4
Over-Two Backstitch

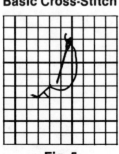

Fig. 5
Over-Two Fill-In Stitch

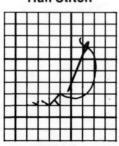

Fig. 6
Over-Three Fill-In Stitch

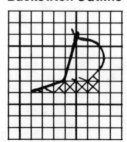

Fig. 7
Over-Three Backstitch
& Fill-In Stitch

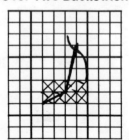

Fig. 8
Two Colors Meeting
with Over-Two Backstitch

Finishing Instructions—Even if your completed stitchery doesn't appear soiled, it is best to hand wash it. Use warm water and mild soap, and handle it as fine lingerie. Rinse it completely and blot excess moisture out with a clean bath towel. Place the stitchery with the floss side down on a clean, dry bath towel, making sure that the threads of the fabric are straight in both directions. Iron on a cotton setting until completely dry. If wool yarns are used in the stitchery project, use the wool setting on the iron. Iron on the back side until completely dry to prevent shrinkage.

Floss-Needed Chart

Symbol	DMC	Susan Bates	Royal Mouline'	Color	Mary	Manger	Shepherd Boy
·	blanc neige	1	1001	white	✔	✔	
6	352	10	2015	salmon	✔	✔	
Ɔ	353	8	2010	light salmon	✔	✔	✔
=	407	883	8255	deep olive flesh			✔
★	413	401	1030	dark gray		✔	✔
I	415	398	1015	medium gray	✔	✔	✔
II	433	358	8215	dark golden-brown	✔		✔
∩	435	309	8210	medium golden-brown	✔	✔	✔
∴	437	362	8205	tan	✔	✔	
——	632	357	8530	brown flesh backstitch	✔	✔	✔
U	676	891	6250	gold			✔
Z	680	901	6260	light golden-brown			✔
#	704	255	5310	light green	✔		
\	712	386	8600	light flesh	✔	✔	
+	726	295	6150	light gold	✔		
4	727	293	6135	light yellow		✔	
O	743	297	6150	medium yellow			✔
♦	746	885	6100	light cream	✔		
C	754	868	8075	dark flesh	✔	✔	
—	762	397	1010	light gray	✔	✔	✔
∴	775	128	4105	ice blue		✔	
$	783	307	6220	dark gold	✔		
♦	801	360	8415	chocolate-brown	✔		✔
L	813	160	4610	sky blue	✔	✔	
●	824	164	4225	deep blue	✔		
N	825	162	4215	dark blue	✔		
×	826	161	4210	medium blue	✔	✔	
∧	827	159	4605	robin-egg blue	✔	✔	
◆	828	158	4850	light blue	✔	✔	
▲	839	358	8560	dark brown		✔	
¢	841	392	8550	medium brown		✔	
:	945	881	8245	medium olive flesh	✔	✔	✔
7	948	778	8070	medium flesh	✔	✔	
V	950	882	8250	dark olive flesh			✔
/	951	778	8240	light olive flesh	✔		✔
∇	3046	886	5810	dark cream	✔		
3	3047	885	5805	medium cream	✔		

Mary and Baby Jesus

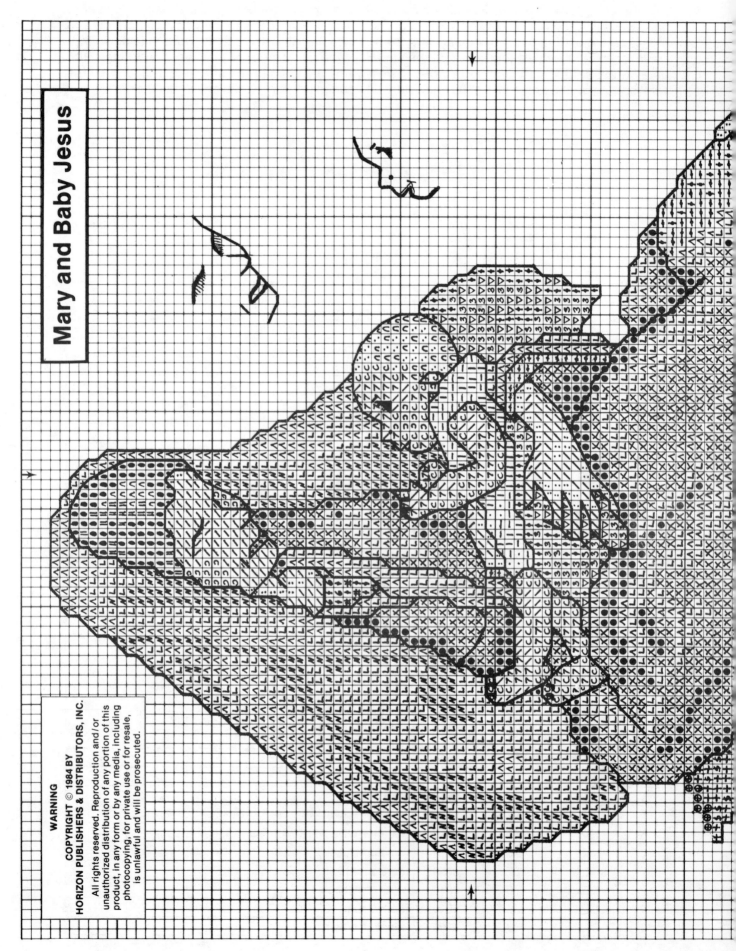

4

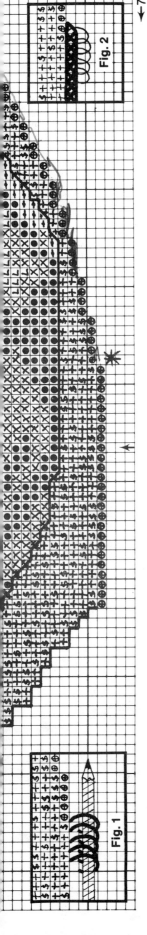

Fig. 1

Fig. 2

89

79

Object	Symbol	DMC	Color Description
Mary's Hair	∩	435	medium golden-brown
	=	433	dark golden-brown
	●	801	chocolate-brown
			801	hair backstitch
Mary's Clothes	♦	828	light blue
	<	827	robin-egg blue
	L	813	sky-blue
	×	826	medium blue
	N	825	dark blue
	●	824	deep blue
	♦	746	light cream
	6	352	salmon
	#	704	light green
			825	veil backstitch
			824	dress backstitch
Shawl on Floor	+	726	light gold
	$	783	dark gold
			783	shawl backstitch
	⊕	726	gold fringe stitch

Object	Symbol	DMC	Color Description
Baby's Flesh	/	712	light flesh
	7	948	medium flesh
	C	754	dark flesh
	◐	353	light salmon
			632	flesh backstitch
			352	salmon backstitch mouth
Baby's Hair	∴	437	tan
	∩	435	medium gold-brown
			435	hair backstitch
Baby's Clothes	·	blanc neige	white
			762	light gray
	—	415	medium gray
			415	clothes backstitch
Baby's Shawl	♦	746	light cream
	3	3047	medium cream
	▷	3046	dark cream
			3046	shawl backstitch
Mary's Flesh	/	712	light flesh
	∴	951	light olive flesh
	◐	945	medium olive flesh
	C	353	light salmon
			632	flesh backstitch
			352	salmon backstitch mouth

Note: To create the appearance of light veil material, use only one strand of floss for all three colors in the veil. Use two strands of floss in the dress.

Fringe Stitch

A three-dimensional fringe stitch on the shawl has been developed for this chart. The stitch should be worked after all the rest of the stitchery is completed.

Make sure the material is stretched tightly in the hoop. Using two strands of DMC #726, anchor the floss at the back of the material. Begin at the ✳ marking. Work from right to left. Bring the floss to the front at the upper right hole of the first ⊕ square. Place a pencil on top of the work, extending horizontally across the bottom of the shawl. Wrap the floss down around the pencil and back into the bottom left corner of that square. Repeat across the shawl for 26 squares, entering each ⊕ square at the upper right corner, taking the floss around the pencil evenly, and exiting to the back of the material at the bottom left corner. (See Figure 1.) The pencil is used to keep the loops the same size. Other household items such as a knitting needle could be used if a smaller loop is desired.

After about twenty loops have been formed, they should be an-chored. To do this, carefully slip the pencil out of the loops and hold them down against the material in an even pattern. With the same floss used for the loops, work a backstitch across the tops of the ⊕ squares, following the diagonals where they occur. Then work a series of cross-stitches back across in each ⊕ square. Finally, backstitch across the bottom of the ⊕ squares. This will anchor the loops securely. (See Figure 2.)

After anchoring the worked loops, the remaining fringe stitches can be worked in groups of about 20, using the pencil and anchoring as directed.

In the other two groups of 20 stitches, the next ⊕ square will often be diagonally down from the previous ⊕ square. The pencil should be allowed to angle diagonally until the next horizontal loops pull it back to the square.

A Shepherd Boy

Object	Symbol	DMC	Color Description
Clothes	O	743	medium yellow
	U	676	gold
	Z	680	light golden-brown
	◗	801	chocolate-brown
	——	801	clothes backstitch
Hair	∩	435	medium golden-brown
	‖	433	dark golden-brown
	◗	801	chocolate-brown
	——	801	hair backstitch
Flesh	╱	951	light olive flesh
	⋮	945	medium olive flesh
	V	950	dark olive flesh
	=	407	deep olive flesh
	⊂	353	light salmon
	——	632	flesh backstitch
Sheep	·	blanc neige	white
	—	762	light gray
	I	415	medium gray
	★	413	dark gray
	——	413	sheep backstitch
	⊙	blanc neige	light gray colonial knots*
	①	415	med. gray colonial knots*

*If colonial knots are not desired, work the areas with regular cross-stitch in the color indicated.

Colonial Knot

The sheep on this chart and the lambs on the "Manger" can be worked with regular cross-stitch. But if a fluffy dimension is desired, the areas marked with circles ⊙ or ① may be worked in colonial knots to give the picture a three-dimensional effect.

The cross-stitches of the entire sheep should be completed first leaving blank the areas marked ⊙ and ①. The outline backstitching should also be completed.

The squares marked ① should be worked first, with the knots in the darker floss establishing the shadows of the animal. Then the remaining squares marked ⊙ should be worked with white floss. This can be done evenly in every square marked ⊙ using 2 strands of floss to create the knot, or the area can be randomly filled in with larger knots using 4 strands of floss. Note: In the model photographed for this book, the sheep with the shepherd boy is worked evenly. The lambs around the manger are worked in the larger knots in a random pattern covering the area.

To Create a Colonial Knot

Anchor the floss at the back of the material which has been stretched tightly in a hoop. Keeping the work face side up, turn it around so you hold it with the shepherd's head closest to your body. The knots will lie better if worked in this position.

Bring the floss to the front of the material in the top of the square to be worked, right next to the backstitching. (See Figure 1.)

With the needle in the right hand, hold the floss to the left and catch the floss with the tip of the needle, moving from left to right. With your left hand, wrap the floss over the end of the needle, creating a figure-eight on top of the needle. (See Figure 2.) This figure-eight twist, instead of merely wrapping the floss around the needle, is the difference between a regular French knot and a colonial knot.

With the floss wrapped around the needle, place the top of the needle into the next hole directly below the first hold. (see Figure 3.)

Pull the floss snugly and draw the knot to the material, making sure you do not pull it through to the back. Cover the area as desired with knots.

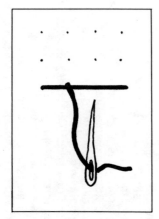

Fig. 1

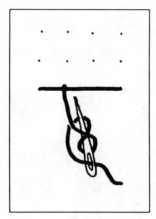

Fig. 2

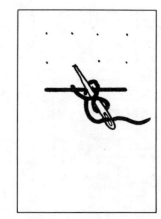

Fig. 3

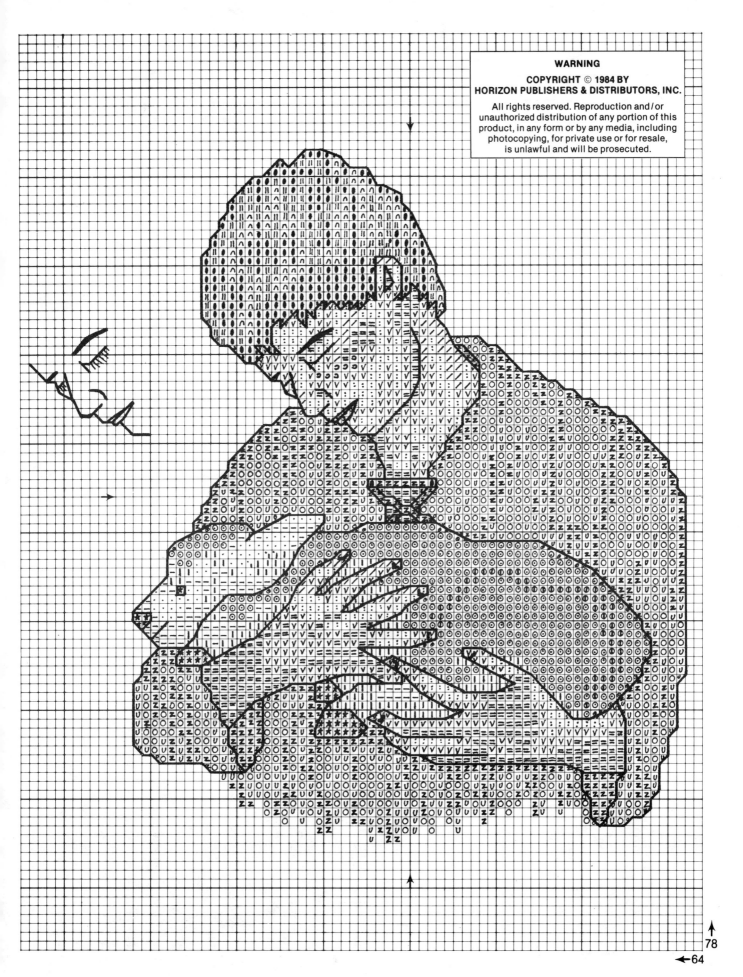

78

←64

The Christ Child in the Manger

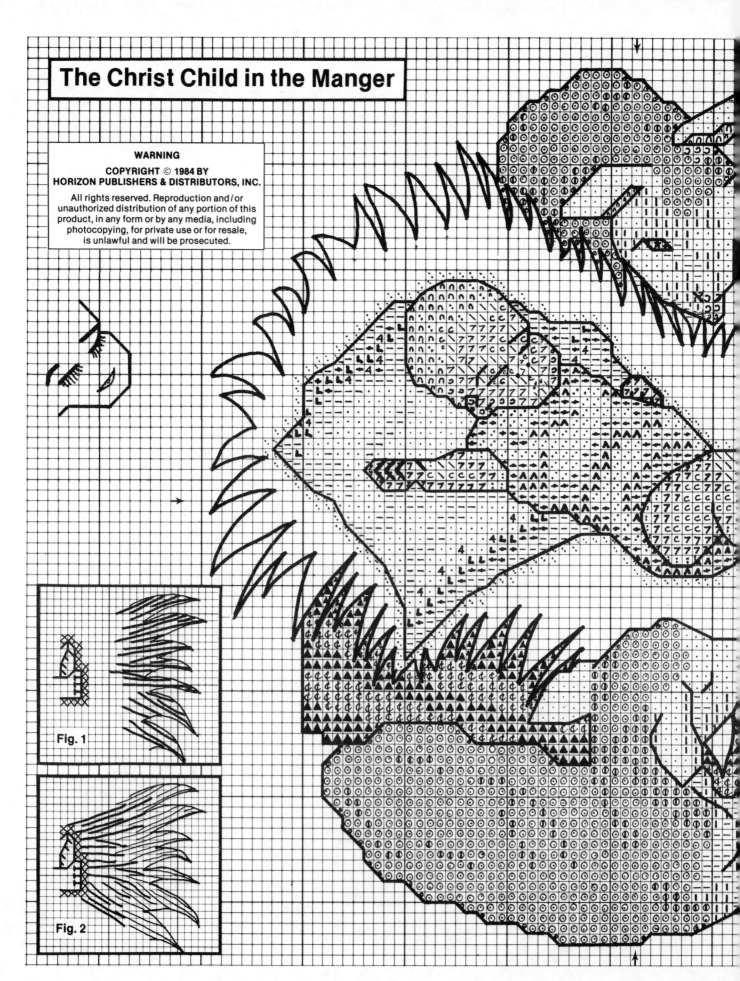

Fig. 1

Fig. 2